Journaling Through the Seasons

Summer & Sonship

Bonnie Liabenow

Journaling through the Seasons
Summer & Sonship

Created by Core Communications International
1443 Newport Street #5
Traverse City, Michigan 49686

Published by Word and Spirit Publishing
PO Box 701403, Tulsa, Oklahoma 74170
wordandspiritpublishing.com

ISBN: 978-1-685730-63-5

Cover design: Bobby Chamberlain, www.bobbycreates.com

Interior design and typeset: Typography Creations

Editor: Mickey Broach

Creative Director & Editor: Meghan Dryzga

Content Advisor: Alyssa Liabenow

Printed in the United States of America.

From the dawn's first golden ray,
To the twilight's gentle sway,
In summer's light, our hearts take flight,
With blessings in each passing day.

The sun awakens, warm and bright,
A whispered prayer in morning's light,
God's hand paints the sky so wide,
Guiding us through time's soft tide.

Gathered 'round in joy and cheer,
With friends and loved ones ever near,
We find contentment in the now,
In every breath, we humbly bow.

Our talents bloom in summer's glow,
Gifts from God that help us grow,
With every skill, with every grace,
We find our path, our rightful place.

We cherish all the work we've done,
The dreams we've chased, the goals we've won,
In every task, His hand we see,
Guiding us to victory.

The laughter shared, the meals made sweet,
The earth beneath our grateful feet,
In these moments, pure and true,
We glimpse the love that He imbues.

From sunrise to the setting sun,
God's presence shines on everyone,
In every breeze, in every song,
His love sustains, so pure, so strong.

As daylight fades to soft twilight,
We rest in peace, the world so right,
For summer's joys are heaven-sent,
A season of pure contentment.

Summertime, the best of dreams,
Where all is more than what it seems,
A time to bask, to simply be,
In God's embrace, eternally free.

With grateful hearts, we seize the day,
Our talents shining on the way,
For in His light, we find success,
A life of love, a life that's blessed.

— UNKNOWN

Contents

Defining the *Season*

> "Like the seasons of nature — winter, spring, summer, and fall — so are the seasons of life. Seasons are specific periods of time, and they vary in length. Some seasons last for a period of years, while others can be just a few short months."
> — *Excellence with Simple Elegance*, p. 102

A summer season of life is represented by the joys of living and is themed, "Sunrise to Sunset."

Sunrise, n.

> "The colors and light visible in the sky on an occasion of the sun's first appearance in the morning." – Cambridge Dictionary

Sunset, n.

> "The time in the evening when the sun disappears and daylight fades." – Cambridge Dictionary

"And God said, 'Let there be light,' and there was light. God saw that the light was good, and he separated the light from the darkness. God called the light 'day,' and the darkness he called 'night'. And there was evening, and there was morning—the first day." – Genesis 1: 3-5 (NIV)

Sonship, n.

> "The position of being a son, especially the son of God in the Christian faith. Christ is the Son of God in the perfect sense of sonship. As the result of our baptism (adoption), we share in Christ's sonship experiencing the joy and privilege of sonship."
> – Cambridge Dictionary

"But when the set time had fully come, God sent his Son, born of a woman, born under the law, to redeem those under the law, so that we might receive adoption to sonship. Because you are his sons, God sent the Spirit of his Son into our hearts, the Spirit who calls 'Abba, Father'. So you are no longer a slave, but God's child; and since you are his child, God has made you also an heir." –Galatians 4: 4-7 (NIV)

"…the Spirit you received brought about your adoption to sonship. And by him we cry, 'Abba, Father.'" – Romans 8:15 (NIV)

"For He chose us in Him before the creation of the world to be holy and blameless in His sight. In love, He predestined us for adoption to sonship through Jesus Christ, in accordance with His pleasure and will – to the praise of His glorious grace, which He has freely given us in the One he loves." – Ephesians 1: 4-6 (NIV)

The *Benefits* of Journaling

Why Journal?

> *As I look through my past journals, I see how God has been working in my life, and that reminds me that He is constantly present.* – Bonnie Liabenow

There's something about writing – something about jotting down how we've felt and what we've learned in a fleeting moment on a day that may have seemed otherwise unremarkable. We so often remember the grandest core memories – where God's work was so evident, he seemingly all but showed up and shook hands around the room. But when life moves, smaller moments move faster, and even the most joyful ones dissipate to join those now forgotten.

Journaling can preserve them. Journaling can capture and preserve the tireless work of God in our everyday lives so that we may reflect, grow and sometimes just find peace in knowing that He's there. Here are some of the benefits you'll notice as you continue this practice:

- **Objective Reflection**: Journaling is a factual account of your journey. This helps us take a more objective look at our lives and our progress, helping us realize that we are indeed moving ahead.
- **A Safe Space for Emotional Expression**: Journaling provides a private, non-judgmental space for emotional expression and exploration. Your journal is one of the few places you don't have to censor yourself or worry about outside reactions to your thoughts.
- **Stress Management**: Journaling can help manage the stress of juggling multiple roles — employee, parent, spouse, caregiver, etc., we have every day. It can help reduce stress by organizing thoughts and problems, making them feel more manageable.
- **Self-Awareness**: Journaling regularly can help us become more aware of our thoughts, feelings, and behaviors. This can lead to better self-understanding, growth, and personal development.
- **Memory and Cognitive Function**: Journaling can enhance memory and cognitive functions. It encourages the brain to dissect experiences and memories, which can lead to improved comprehension and recall.
- **Healing**: Journaling has been used as a tool in therapeutic settings and for self-help, as writing about traumas or negative experiences can help in the healing process.
- **Empowerment**: Journaling allows each of us to express our personal experiences, ideas, and views freely. It can be a tool for empowerment, helping each of us find our voice in a society where we may feel unheard.

- **Goal Setting and Personal Growth:** Journaling can assist in setting and tracking goals; it can be a great tool for personal growth, helping to monitor progress over time.

HOW WILL THIS HELP ME GROW IN MY FAITH?

> *When you reflect on how good God is—and all the great things He has done, is doing, and even will do in your life—there's a natural sense of gratefulness. Documenting these moments protects you from ever taking for granted the love and mercy of God in your life—the moments that so quickly fade are great blessings, and they are enough to keep us amazed.* – BONNIE LIABENOW

The habit of journaling can strengthen your spiritual walk as it encourages you to dedicate time to your faith, beliefs, and spiritual insights. Your journal allows you to identify what is starving your spirit and brings quietness to a busy day.

WHERE DO I START?

> *I write down verses that encourage me, some of the prayer requests I'm praying that day, things I feel like the Lord is putting on my heart, and the good things that God does for me. If I want to hear God speak to me, the first thing I do is say, "God, I want you to speak to me. Hearing from you is not just nice, it is a necessity!" And then I withdraw and get alone and quiet. ("Be still and know that I am God.") And then I wait quietly, patiently, and expectantly on God. I ask a specific question, I look into his Word and then when I see God's answer, I write it down. Habakkuk said, "The Lord gave me this answer, 'Write down clearly… what I reveal to you…'"* – BONNIE LIABENOW

Choose one of the topics below that resonates most with you. Start small so you don't feel overwhelmed, and take it just one sentence at a time. Length of entry doesn't matter – only your authenticity. You can:

- Write about the goodness of God in your life!
- Write about a tough situation when God has protected and guided you.
- Keep a record of your petitions and blessings.
- Make it a gratitude journal of your words of praise and worship using the different names for God provided in the prompts given.

Not every day will look the same, and that's welcomed and expected.

Tips for Journaling

- **Redefine journaling.** This is not the same as keeping a diary. A diary is, 'Dear diary, this is what I did today.' A journal is, 'This is what I learned today.'
- **Write spiritual encounters.** If it's on your heart, don't hesitate to write it down. All spiritual encounters with the most Holy God are worthy of documenting.
- **Write your heartfelt response.** Start by reading scripture (each psalm) two or three times with the prayerful question in mind: *What does God want me to hear, read, or see from this? How does this resonate with me? As I meditate on the words, what stands out? Does it provide answers? Does it raise questions?* Or *does it not resonate at all, and why?* Ask God for clarity in these lines.
- **Same time.** Set a time each day to sit and self-reflect on your journey. You may look at how you are feeling and

examine why you feel that way. You can also write down things that inspire you throughout the day.

- **Read for inspiration.** Reading your daily writing can help you work toward new goals, search for more answers to questions you've had in the last month, and give thanks for the lessons you've already learned.
- **Set goals.** Setting goals can inspire you. These can be things you wish to do on a daily basis to further your personal growth or things you hope to do within a certain amount of time. Refer to *Excellence with Simple Elegance, Chapter: Goal Setting, Page 145* and also *The Study* for more guidance.
- **Practice gratitude.** It helps to create a thankful heart. Acknowledge your blessings. Write about the things in your day that make you feel grateful. Research shows that people who make a point to feel gratitude are happier and healthier people.
- **Document.** Write down accounts in which you see God working in your life like answers to prayers, and God's favor and blessings given to you. Journaling brings awareness of God's presence in our life, especially that God shows up in both Big ways and small blessings.
- **Take it with you.** Keep your journal with you at all times. Keeping your journal on hand allows you to write down quotes, spiritual text references, or general thoughts you wish to reflect on right when they come to mind.
- **Look back.** Review your journal entries at least once a month. By taking time to self-reflect on your prior entries, you can better see the direction you're heading in spiritual enlightenment.

- **Be authentic.** The Book of Psalms is a great example of journal writing. David took the first five books of the Bible: Genesis, Exodus, Leviticus, Numbers, Deuteronomy, and he meditated on them day and night and wrote his prayers down. As you read the Psalms, you'll see that David includes just about every emotion known to the human race including envy, jealousy, lust, and greed. David is brutally honest in his writing; he does not write what he thinks, he writes what he honestly feels. This paves a path of authenticity, setting a powerful example for us in our own journaling.
- **Enjoy It.**

A Note on *Summer* and Its *Sunrise to Sunset*

By Meghan Dryzga

"What if it all works out?" Sunlight shone in through the door-wall, cascaded across the arm of the sofa, and stretched to reach the edge of the coffee table in the middle of the room. My heart swelled, my eyes welled up, and I knew God was trying to reach me. "What if it all works out?" The words were framed and centered on the wall of my oldest daughter's new apartment; a necessary approach, perhaps, as His subtler reminders hadn't quite shaken me awake.

When the world is swirling, and we're distracted by its chaos, look for the sun. *The Son. Summer is here. It's right here.* Sometimes we need reminders. Sometimes there are years between our prayers and their outcomes. But look for the summer. It's here.

Without mulling over familial details, I'll simply say, the co-parenting journey can be challenging. It was for us. When I met my husband, he had a toddler whose mother had moved her states away; and when we married, without hesitation, we moved to her. *We made all the right choices.* We relocated to a state we didn't choose, and we did it without our own families or a network of friends to support us. It was hard. *We made all the right decisions, sacrifices, prioritizing what was best for our daughter.* And, at times, this journey – when you don't have a voice, when you're not consulted, when your time is limited, when you have to return your child to a house that's not yours and you're not ready to miss her again – even all the right decisions can feel thankless.

Of course, there were beautiful moments strung throughout the journey, each infused with summer's Sonshine. But when so much feels out of your control, even memories are glazed with a sense of helplessness. *Am I making a difference in her life?* You wonder. *Will any of this matter to her?* Distracted by my own emotions, I know I missed the beauty in some of life's most meaningful milestones.

As she progressed through high school and college, I most wanted to show her life outside this little town she'd been raised in. I wanted her to taste independence and thrive. I wanted her to stretch and see and know and feel confidence in herself... to feel pride in the ability to pave her own path beyond this place. In fact, I wanted this so much for her that I set her up with a summer internship in a big city. "THIS IS IT," I thought. "It's happening!" I packed my proverbial summer gear into my heart's suitcase, and prepared myself to share the good news.

My heart leapt when she got the offer. I was so eager for proof she'd find success. But, I should know, you can't force a God Thing. We're reminded in a Time for Everything (Ecclesiastes) that summer Son shines in His timing. And, when our daughter declined (declined!) the internship offer, it clearly wasn't His timing. Yet.

So, months later, when she sat on the sofa with her heels firmly planted in her new apartment with her new job in her big new city, it was the sign above her head that caught my eye. "What if it all works out?" It made sense; there were years of summer seasons to celebrate, but I scarcely acknowledged them to the degree they were awarded. So it made sense why it took a giant sign – a literal, giant sign – to alert me of the season that had arrived.

And I think it's *that* – *that* chance we may move too quickly through the warmth of His summer season or even not notice the beauty of it at all – is why this journal is so important.

Life is fast and relentless. But the sun still shines upon us, and through Bonnie's reflections in the pages ahead, we won't miss a thing. You'll learn to recognize and embrace every corner of this brilliant, joyful season; you'll practice being present and leaning into each moment so you become mindful and acutely aware of His presence. You'll describe the feeling of the sun on your face, and sit in it. Just sit. *This one's my favorite.*

See, we're coached in life to be humble, to not gloat, and to not show intense joyful emotions – perhaps so we don't offend or draw envy from the people around us. So, when I feel an overwhelming sense of joy, I often quickly look beyond it. Knowing that euphoria won't last forever, my brain uses logic to protect me from future disappointment; I either question the reality of the joyful situation, or dismiss it quicker than it deserves. I've missed remarkable summer seasons on account of this response. Just last summer, after years and years of soccer training without recognition, my son found a coach who gave him confidence and a deeply rewarding fall season. And yet, the gratitude and elation I felt for him was quickly replaced by anxiety about when it would end or which team may be out to crush his freshly renewed spirit. *How wild!* What a wild habit we've formed to protect ourselves by denying the depths of joy we feel when summer comes.

If you've found yourself in a similar routine, I have exciting news: With the guidance in Summer & Sonship, this summer promises to be transformational. Bonnie encourages us with scripture and songs of joy and praise to remember how God wants us to experience His brightest season – in nature, through our work, and within ourselves. Of course, joy tends to replicate in fellowship, so you'll reflect on how to recognize, infuse and breathe summer into your relationships. And, so you can see where God's been in summers past, you'll practice pulling moments of Sonshine from your memories. There's so much not to miss.

You know, it's funny how, in the wake of the slightest breeze, the warmth of the sun – the Son – can give you goosebumps. That day, as I stood in the path of the doorwall in my daughter's apartment, rays of sun warmed my skin, and I felt the foreverness of joy in His presence. "What if it all works out?," the Lord whispered. And it had, hadn't it... Just like He promised. It was summer in the city, and the Sonshine was bright.

A Summer Song of *Worship* and *Praise*

Inspired By Psalm 66 & 72

Song of Praise and Thanks to God

Raise the voice of joy to God, all the earth! Sing out the honor of His name! Make His praise great!

Sing songs to the tune of His glory
Set glory to the rhythms of His praise

I will honor the Lord for His glory and His strength. I will honor the Lord for the glory of His name, worshiping Him in the splendor of His holiness. God keeps me alive and keeps my feet on solid ground. He has tested me, making me pure as silver. He has blessed me with much more than I could ever need. In response to His goodness, I will come into His house with my offering, returning a portion of what He has given to me.

Praise His glorious name!

Let the whole earth be filled with His glory!

At sunrise, let the mountains give exuberant witness of His glory and the hills flourish with righteousness.

The Lord is faithful to give me strength when in need. He will keep me alive and will keep my feet on solid ground. The Lord will bless me with peace.

Praise His glorious name forever!

Let the whole earth be filled with His glory!
Be refreshing like summer rain,
Let righteousness burst into blossom
And peace abounds until sunset.

I will tell you what He has done for me. I will cry out to Him with my mouth and praise Him with my voice. I am aware that the Lord will not hear me if I hold on to the sin in my heart. So I daily ask forgiveness to be sure that God has heard. I am so thankful to God who forgives, for He has listened to my prayers. My heart's desire is to forever honor You and thank You, my God.

Praise be to the Lord God, the God of Israel, who alone does such wonderful things.

Response:

A Summer Song of *Worship* and *Praise*

Highlight and respond below

INSPIRED BY PSALM 66 & 72

Song of Praise and Thanks to God

RAISE the voice of joy to God, all the earth! Sing out the honor of His name! Make His praise great!

Sing songs to the tune of His glory
Set glory to the rhythms of His praise

I will honor the Lord for His glory and His strength. I will honor the Lord for the glory of His name, worshiping Him in the splendor of His holiness.

God keeps me alive and keeps my feet on solid ground. He has tested me, making me pure as silver.

He has blessed me with much more than I could ever need. In response to His goodness, I will come into His house with my offering, returning a portion of what He has given to me.

Praise His glorious name!
Let the whole earth be filled with His glory!

At sunrise, let the mountains give exuberant witness of His glory and the hills flourish with righteousness.

The Lord is faithful to give me strength when in need. He will keep me alive and will keep my feet on solid ground. The Lord will bless me with peace.

Praise His glorious name forever!
Let the whole earth be filled with His glory!

Be refreshing like summer rain,
Let righteousness burst into blossom
And peace abounds until sunset.

I will tell you what He has done for me. I will cry out to Him with my mouth and praise Him with my voice. I am aware that the Lord will not hear me if I hold on to the sin in my heart. So I daily ask forgiveness to be sure that God has heard. I am so thankful to God who forgives, for He has listened to my prayers. My heart's desire is to forever honor You and thank You, my God.

Praise be to the Lord God, the God of Israel, who alone does such wonderful things.

Reflection:

"Summertime is always the best of what might be."
– Charles Bowden

My excitement over entering into a summer season in my life – the richness of all God did in my life to change me, refine me, teach me – is evident in the season I am leaving and the new one I am entering into. I cannot tell you what being a mother of young children did for me and how being an entrepreneur has changed me over the years and caused me to grow. Birthing vision and engaging in radical faith causes you to become a better person – a seasoned person. It took faith to do everything I've done.

As I move into this season, I take everything I've learned with me and everything God brought into my life to stretch me till I thought I could be stretched no more; I combine that with the gifts He's given me, and I'm ready to run into all He's called me to do.

I say "yes," to anything and everything God has for me in this next season. Am I afraid? Of course. Am I struggling not knowing exactly what that looks like? Of course! I would not be human if I said anything else. However, this past season has prepared me to walk into the future with rest and great confidence knowing He will direct my path, He will give me the wisdom to forge ahead with strength, and the ability to deeply love those who join me in the journey. I'm ready! Let's do this! – Michelle

Emotional Expression:

Joy in the Best of Times

Use the sunshine images provided to respond to the prompts.

The richness of all God did in your life to change you, refine you, and teach you is evident in the season you are leaving, allowing you to celebrate the new joyful summer season you are entering. Write 10 words that best describe your feelings as you step into this season defined as *the best of what might be*.

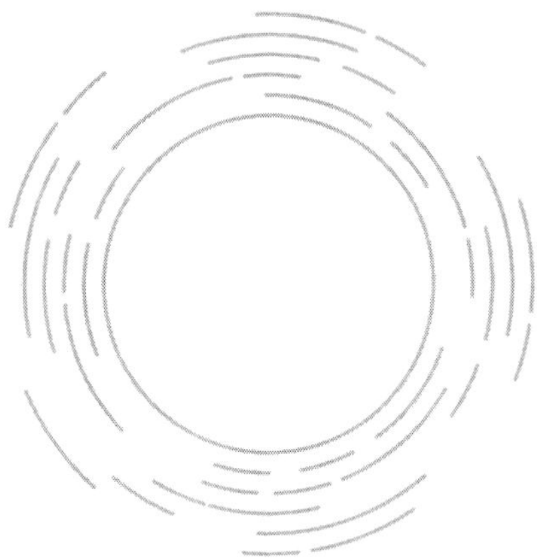

Past seasons have prepared you to walk into this joyful season with:

- Great confidence that God will direct your path
- Wisdom to forge ahead with strength
- Ability to deeply love those who join you in the journey

Express how you plan to celebrate the joys of living. Use each descriptive phrase to inspire thoughts around the best of times.

I take everything learned with me.

I take everything God brought into my life to stretch me.

I come with the gifts God has given me.

I walk into this wonderful season of celebration with rest and great confidence.

Notes

Notes

Notes

Notes

A Summer Prayer of *Petition* and *Blessing*

Jehovah-Shammah — Present

"I will never leave you or let you be alone." — Hebrews 13:5

Be happy in the Lord, for He is present, and He will give you the desires of your heart.

I will trust in the Lord and seek His goodness daily. His promises I will embrace. I will enjoy living well in His beautiful land and I will be well nourished. I am happy living His way for He knows my every desire.

Oh sweet friend, give your way over to the Lord. Trust in Him and He will make you as the light and your wise actions as the noonday. Rest in the Lord and be willing to wait for Him. Do not be like those who do wrong, for they will soon dry up like the grass. Like the green plant, they will soon die. But God and His promises are forever.

Do not trouble yourself when all goes well with the one who carries out his sinful plans. Stop being angry. Turn away from fighting; it leads only to wrongdoing. But those who wait for the Lord will be given the desire of their hearts. In a little while, the sinful one will be no more. You will look for their place and they will not be there. But those who put their trust in God will enjoy eternal happiness and have much more than they could ever need.

I will be happy living God's way and will take comfort that He knows the desires within my heart.

I will trust in the Lord and seek His goodness. I will enjoy His beautiful land.

I will find peace resting and waiting. I have given my ways over to the Lord and trusted Him. My being right and good is shown as the light and my wise actions as the noonday. The few belongings of those right with God are surely better than the riches of the ungodly. For the Lord guides each step I take, and I willingly follow. In this obedience, I experience all His love, goodness and kindness.

Oh sweet friend, turn from sin and do good so you will live forever and experience the true joy of your salvation. For the Lord loves what is fair and right. He does not leave the people alone who belong to Him; they are kept forever. The mouth of the one who is right with God speaks wisdom, and their tongue speaks what is fair and good. The Law of his God is in their hearts; His steps do not leave it. Wait for the Lord. Keep His way. He will give you a high place and you will find strength in Him during times of trouble.

I will trust in the Lord and will seek His goodness daily. His promises I will embrace. I will enjoy living well in His beautiful land, and I will be well nourished.

I am happy living His way, for He knows my every desire and will never leave me.

Response:

A Summer Prayer of *Petition* and *Blessing*

Highlight and respond below

INSPIRED BY PSALM 37

Jehovah-Shammah – Present

“I will never leave you or let you be alone.” – HEBREWS 13:5

BE happy in the Lord, for He is present, and He will give you the desires of your heart.

I will trust in the Lord and seek His goodness daily. His promises I will embrace. I will enjoy living well in His beautiful land and I will be well nourished.

I am happy living His way for He knows my every desire.

Oh sweet friend, give your way over to the Lord. Trust in Him and He will make you as the light and your wise actions as the noonday. Rest in the Lord and be willing to wait for Him. Do not be like those who do wrong, for they will soon dry up like the grass. Like the green plant, they will soon die. But God and His promises are forever.

Do not trouble yourself when all goes well with the one who carries out his sinful plans. Stop being angry. Turn away from fighting. It leads only to wrongdoing. But those who wait for the Lord will be given the desire of their hearts. In a little while, the sinful one will be no more. You will look for their place and they will not be there. But those who put their trust in God will enjoy eternal happiness and have much more than they could ever need.

I will be happy living God's way and will take comfort that He knows the desires within my heart.

I will trust in the Lord and seek His goodness. I will enjoy His beautiful land. I will find peace resting and waiting. I have given my ways over to the Lord and trusted Him. My being right and good is shown as the light and my wise actions as the noonday. The few belongings of those right with God are surely better than the riches of the ungodly. For the Lord guides each step I take, and I willingly follow. In this obedience, I experience all His love, goodness and kindness.

Oh sweet friend, turn from sin and do good so you will live forever and experience the true joy of your salvation. For the Lord loves what is fair and right. He does not leave the people alone who belong to Him; they are kept forever. The mouth of the one who is right with God speaks wisdom, and their tongue speaks what is fair and good. The Law of his God is in their hearts; His steps do not leave it. Wait for the Lord. Keep His way. He will give you a high place and you will find strength in Him during times of trouble.

I will trust in the Lord and will seek His goodness daily. His promises I will embrace. I will enjoy living well in His beautiful land, and I will be well nourished.

I am happy living His way, for He knows my every desire and will never leave me.

Reflection:

♪♪♪ ***Sonship***

I wanna hear a song from heaven
That comes directly from Your heart
I wanna cry the tears of beauty
Of when You leave me mesmerized

Lord I know that You saved me already
But I need You to save me every day
Open arms on my knees
I am ready
Take over my heart

You heal and nourish and satisfy
Divine exchange sunrise to sunset
Replacing with truth all the lies

I'm not an orphan
You wrap Your arms around me
I'm not alone
Wherever You go I go
I wanna hear your voice

– lyrics by KAREN JULI

"Happiness cannot be traveled to, owned, earned, worn or consumed. Happiness is the spiritual experience of living every minute with love, grace and gratitude." – DENIS WAITLEY

Self Awareness:

Joy in Being Present

It's a challenge to stay present and allow for the celebration. It's sometimes difficult to slow down the hustle in order to fully immerse in a season of goodness. Ponder these two questions: Are you fully conscious of this present moment? Is your mind free from the noise of internal dialogue or the thoughts of the past and future to appreciate the happiness that's before you at this moment?

Being present is a skill that requires practice and intentionality. Anything worth doing takes practice to be proficient. But you'll soon realize the practice is time well spent.

We'll start this practice in the exercise below.

Read the Sonship lyrics again, paying special attention to the underlined phrases. What's the songwriter asking for? Imagine you are the songwriter; what would the underlined phrases represent in your life? Think about these phrases as they relate to living fully aware and present. What might these words represent as you strive to be present and mindful, every minute, of His love, grace, mercy, and gratitude. After each set of lyrics, respond to the prompts with your thoughts.

Living Every Minute With God's Love

♪♪♪ *I wanna hear a song from heaven*
That comes directly from Your heart
I wanna cry the tears of beauty
Of when You leave me mesmerized

The place of beauty that brings tears to my eyes and leaves me mesmerized is ______________________________

____

____.

Living Every Minute By God's Grace

♪♪♪ *Lord I know that You saved me already*

The day of my salvation was ______________________

____.

But I need You to save me every day

So that I may ____________________________________

____.

Open arms on my knees
I am ready
Take over my heart

My heart needs __________________________________

____.

Living Every Minute In God's Mercy

♪♪♪ *You heal and nourish and satisfy*
Divine exchange sunrise to sunset
Replacing with truth all the lies

The blessings that nourish me as I wake to the sunrise are

____

____.

At sunset, remembering God's promises that satisfy me are

____

____.

Living Every Minute With Gratitude

♪♪♪ *I'm not an orphan*
You wrap Your arms around me

I'm grateful for your embrace during moments of ________

____

____.

I'm not alone
Wherever You go I go
I wanna hear your voice

I desperately need to hear your voice when I am __________

____

____.

A Prayer for Presence

Use this space to write a prayer. You might write something like, "God, give me a bright awareness of Your presence in my life and give me an active desire to stay present in this moment. Remember it and recite it across the day to make presence of mind a habit.

Notes

Notes

Notes

A Summer Song of *Worship* and *Praise*

Inspired By Psalm 1, 8 & 9

God, Brilliant Lord, Yours is a Household Name.

I'm thanking You, God, from a full heart. I'm whistling, laughing and jumping for joy; I'm singing Your song, O Lord. You took over and set everything right; when I needed You, You were there, taking charge.

You see and set the world's mess right. You decide what is right for us and will never leave us alone. You are a safe house, a sanctuary during bad times. The moment I arrive in Your sanctuary, I feel safe. I relax and am never sorry I knocked and entered into Your presence.

O Lord, my Lord, how great is Your name in all the earth. You have set Your shining greatness above the heavens. I look up and think about Your heavens, the work of Your fingers, the moon and the stars, which You have set in their places. Who am I but an ordinary person? Yet you, the God of heaven, think me worthy of your care and goodness.

Out of the mouths of children and babies; nursing infants sing their choruses to You; toddlers shout their songs. You made us a little less than the angels. You made us to rule over the works of Your hands. You put all things under our feet: all sheep and cattle, all the wild animals, the birds of the air, the fish of the sea and all that pass through the sea.

O Lord, our Lord, how great is Your name in all the earth. I will shout the songs with the children and praise Your holy name. Your presence in my life brings me great joy.

Continue to be kind to me, God. I've been kicked around long enough. You've pulled me back from the gates of death, and I now have joy. I'll write the book on hallelujahs on the corner of Main and First. I'll hold a street meeting; I'll be the song leader; we'll fill the air with salvation songs. Genuine happiness comes to the one who does not walk in a sinful way or stand in the path of sinners or sit with those who laugh at the truth.

Everlasting joy is in You, Lord, and I am mindful day and night of Your goodness to me. I am like a tree planted by rivers of water, which gives its fruit at the right time; its leaves never dry up. My household is blessed, and I am confident that whatever I do will work out well for me; for You, Lord, have found favor with my household.

I'm thanking You, God, from a full heart. I'm whistling, laughing and jumping for joy; I'm singing Your song, O Lord. For You, O Lord, know the way of those who are right with You. And I am thankful, for Your presence in my life brings me great joy.

Response:

A Summer Song of *Worship* and *Praise*

Highlight and respond below

Inspired By Psalm 1, 8 & 9

God, Brilliant Lord, Yours is a Household Name.

I'm thanking You, God, from a full heart. I'm whistling, laughing and jumping for joy; I'm singing Your song, O Lord. You took over and set everything right; when I needed You, You were there, taking charge.

You see and set the world's mess right. You decide what is right for us and will never leave us alone. You are a safe house, a sanctuary during bad times. The moment I arrive in Your sanctuary, I feel safe. I relax and am never sorry I knocked and entered into Your presence.

O Lord, my Lord, how great is Your name in all the earth. You have set Your shining greatness above the heavens. I look up and think about Your heavens, the work of Your fingers, the moon and the stars, which You have set in their places. Who am I but an ordinary person? Yet you, the God of heaven, think me worthy of your care and goodness.

Out of the mouths of children and babies; nursing infants sing their choruses to You; toddlers shout their songs. You made us a little less than the angels. You made us to rule over the works of Your hands. You put all things under our feet: all sheep and cattle, all the wild animals, the birds of the air, the fish of the sea and all that pass through the sea.

O Lord, our Lord, how great is Your name in all the earth. I will shout the songs with the children and praise Your holy name. Your presence in my life brings me great joy.

Continue to be kind to me, God. I've been kicked around long enough. You've pulled me back from the gates of death, and I now have joy. I'll write the book on hallelujahs on the corner of Main and First. I'll hold a street meeting; I'll be the song leader; we'll fill the air with salvation songs. Genuine happiness comes to the one who does not walk in a sinful way or stand in the path of sinners or sit with those who laugh at the truth.

Everlasting joy is in You, Lord, and I am mindful day and night of Your goodness to me. I am like a tree planted by rivers of water, which gives its fruit at the right time; its leaves never dry up. My household is blessed, and I am confident that whatever I do will work out well for me; for You, Lord, have found favor with my household.

I'm thanking You, God, from a full heart. I'm whistling, laughing and jumping for joy; I'm singing Your song, O Lord. For You, O Lord, know the way of those who are right with You. And I am thankful, for Your presence in my life brings me great joy.

Reflection:

"When you love what you have, you have everything you need."
– UNKNOWN

"Happiness isn't about having the best of everything. It's about seeing the best in everything." – JANE LEE LOGAN

Gratitude:

Joy in Contentment

Use the sunshine images provided to respond to the prompts.

Scripture tells us that godliness with contentment is our greatest gain.

This verse in 1 Timothy 6:6 suggests that true wealth comes with a combination of godliness and contentment. We are reassured, then, that wealth isn't about material possessions and earthly things – as that's all temporary. Contentment is about who you have, not what you have. This song of Psalm reminds us that everlasting joy comes with God's presence in our life.

As you reflect on your current state of being, list life's gains that are delivering joy.

"Contentment is a state of being in which one is satisfi ed with their current situation and the state of affairs in one's life as they presently are. If one is content, they are pleased with their situation and how the elements in one's life are situated. A sense of peace... a feeling of quiet happiness and satisfaction..." – COLLINS ENGLISH DICTIONARY

Reflect on the definition of contentment. In your life, what is satisfying? What brings peace and a sense of quiet happiness?

Where do you feel happiness in your body? How does joy show up physically for you?

"Out of the mouths of children and babies; nursing infants sing their choruses to You; toddlers shout their songs." Often children deliver infectious joy. This song of Psalm reminds us as they find contentment with ease, and we tend to match their standard in their presence. "I will shout the songs with the children and praise Your holy name."

What is the source of your joyful mood right now? What infectious influence brings undeniable contentment in this moment?

How are you making room for more of those joyful influences in your daily life?

Notes

Notes

Notes

A Summer Prayer of *Petition* and *Blessing*

Inspired By Psalm 119

Jehovah-Chereb – Lord the Sword

"He is your excellent sword!" – Deuteronomy 33:29

O, how I love Your Word! It is what I think about all through the day. Your Word makes me wiser. I have a better understanding because I obey Your Word. How sweet is Your Word to my taste! It is sweeter than honey to my mouth!

Your Word is a lamp to my feet and a light to my path.

O Lord, Your Word will never change in heaven. I will never forget Your Word for, by it, You have given me new life. I have seen that all things have an end, even if they are perfect, but Your Word is without end.

With Your very own hands, you formed me; now please breathe Your wisdom over me so I can understand You. Train me in good common sense; I'm thoroughly committed to living Your way.

I can see now, God, that Your decisions are right; Your testing has taught me what's true and right. Oh, love me—right now—and hold me tight! Comfort me so I can live, really live; Your revelation is the tune that makes me dance. Before I learned to answer You, I wandered all over the place, but now I'm in step with Your Word. You are good, and the source of good; train me in Your goodness.

Your Word I have hidden in my heart that I might not sin against You.

Let your love, God, shape my life. Then, I'll be able to stand up to mockery because I trusted Your Word. Don't ever deprive me of truth, not ever; Your commandments are what I depend on. Oh, I'll guard with my life what You have revealed to me. Your truth and Your wisdom are precious and I will guard them both forever.

I'll tell the world what I find, speak out boldly in public, unembarrassed. I cherish Your Word—oh, how I love it—relishing every fragment of Your counsel. Teach me, O Lord, the way of Your statutes, and I will keep it to the end. Give me understanding and I will observe it with my whole heart. Help me walk in the path of righteousness, for I delight in it. Incline my heart to Your testimonies and not to covetousness. Turn away my eyes from looking at worthless things, and revive me in Your way. Establish Your Word in me, for I long for Your precepts. Revive me with Your righteousness.

Your Word is a lamp to my feet and a light to my path.

Blessed are You, O Lord! Teach me Your ways. With my lips I have declared all the judgements of Your mouth. I have rejoiced in the way of Your testimonies, as much as in all riches. I will delight myself in Your statutes; I will not forget Your Word.

Response:

A Summer Prayer of *Petition* and *Blessing*

Highlight and respond below

Inspired By Psalm 119

Jehovah-Chereb – Lord the Sword

"He is your excellent sword!" – Deuteronomy 33:29

O, how I love Your Word! It is what I think about all through the day. Your Word makes me wiser. I have a better understanding because I obey Your Word. How sweet is Your Word to my taste! It is sweeter than honey to my mouth!

Your Word is a lamp to my feet and a light to my path.

O Lord, Your Word will never change in heaven. I will never forget Your Word for, by it, You have given me new life. I have seen that all things have an end, even if they are perfect, but Your Word is without end.

With Your very own hands, you formed me; now please breathe Your wisdom over me so I can understand You. Train me in good common sense; I'm thoroughly committed to living Your way.

I can see now, God, that Your decisions are right; Your testing has taught me what's true and right. Oh, love me—right now—and hold me tight! Comfort me so I can live, really live; Your revelation is the tune that makes me dance.

Before I learned to answer You, I wandered all over the place, but now I'm in step with Your Word. You are good, and the source of good; train me in Your goodness.

Your Word I have hidden in my heart that I might not sin against You.

Let your love, God, shape my life. Then, I'll be able to stand up to mockery because I trusted Your Word. Don't ever deprive me of truth, not ever; Your commandments are what I depend on. Oh, I'll guard with my life what You have revealed to me. Your truth and Your wisdom are precious and I will guard them both forever.

I'll tell the world what I find, speak out boldly in public, unembarrassed. I cherish Your Word—oh, how I love it—relishing every fragment of Your counsel. Teach me, O Lord, the way of Your statutes, and I will keep it to the end. Give me understanding and I will observe it with my whole heart.

Help me walk in the path of righteousness, for I delight in it. Incline my heart to Your testimonies and not to covetousness. Turn away my eyes from looking at worthless things, and revive me in Your way. Establish Your Word in me, for I long for Your precepts. Revive me with Your righteousness.

Your Word is a lamp to my feet and a light to my path.

Blessed are You, O Lord! Teach me Your ways. With my lips I have declared all the judgements of Your mouth. I have rejoiced in the way of Your testimonies, as much as in all riches. I will delight myself in Your statutes; I will not forget Your Word.

Reflection:

"Let every man abide in the calling wherein he is called and his work will be as sacred as the work of ministry. It is not what man does that determines whether his work is sacred or secular, it is why he does it." – A.W. Toser

"God will use your abilities and talents to touch others powerfully, when your heart is to give to others from what God has given you." – Stormie Omartian

Personal Growth:

Joy in Accomplishment

Carrying your God-given talents into your workday makes the day so rewarding. Identify and circle your God-given talents from the list; reflect on the strengths that you're able to share through the work you do – as they are the ones that can bring the most fulfillment to each day.

Ethical	Willingness to Learn
Problem Solver	Patient
Confident	Honest
Ambitious	Emotional Intelligence
Good Communicator	Strong Leader
Optimistic	Team Player
Effective Interpersonal Skills	Creative
Reliable	Dedicated
Integrity	Independent
Tolerant	Passionate
Hard Working	Detail Oriented

For each God-given strength and ability you've identified, share how it's an attributing factor to why you love the work you do. To help focus your writing, gain inspiration from some of the benefits of joining work with your talents from the list. How does bringing your talents to your daily work deliver more pleasure, facilitate deeper engagement, or bring more meaning to your work?

Pleasure
(Doing what you enjoy)

Engagement
(Interested & connected)

Meaning
(Feeling like what you do matters)

As Omartian says, *God will use your abilities and talents to touch the lives of others.* So, it's true your work is a ministry – your ministry. No matter what vocation you're committed to, you serve others in some fashion. Treasure the wonderful skill set, talents and wisdom God has given you that you share with others daily. And enjoy your work as you let others experience His goodness through you.

Write a synopsis about your workday and the joy you experience sharing His Sonshine as you serve others.

____

____

____

____

____

____

____

It is not what man does that determines whether his work is sacred or secular, it is ***why*** *he does it.*

Let the **why** keep you motivated to finish strong to your calling each day. What is your Why?

____

____

____

____

____

____

____

Notes

Notes

Notes

A Summer Song of *Worship* and *Praise*

Inspired By Psalm 100

Jehovah – The Lord, God All-powerful – Exodus 6:2

Song of Praise

Heavenly Father, You are my daily celebration. I will invite everyone to join me as I stand to my feet and shout with joy!

Serving You, Lord, brings a smile to my face and the gift of laughter to my soul.

And as I gladly serve You, I will sing songs of joy as I reflect upon the truth that You are God to all people. It is You, Lord, who made us, not us.

We are Your people and the sheep of Your field.

Each day, as I enter Your gates and come into Your holy place, I will praise You and give thanks. I will give honor to Your Holy name in everything I do.

God, You are so good to me. I am comforted in knowing that Your loving kindness lasts forever. You are faithful to me and to my family. I give You all my praise because You are every joy, every triumph, and every good thing in my life.

You are Jehovah, the Lord, God all-powerful.

Response:

A Summer Song of *Worship* and *Praise*

Highlight and respond below

Inspired By Psalm 100

Jehovah – The Lord, God All-powerful – Exodus 6:2

Song of Praise

Heavenly Father, You are my daily celebration. I will invite everyone to join me as I stand to my feet and shout with joy!

Serving You, Lord, brings a smile to my face and the gift of laughter to my soul.

And as I gladly serve You, I will sing songs of joy as I reflect upon the truth that You are God to all people. It is You, Lord, who made us, not us.

We are Your people and the sheep of Your field.

Each day, as I enter Your gates and come into Your holy place, I will praise You and give thanks. I will give honor to Your Holy name in everything I do.

God, You are so good to me. I am comforted in knowing that Your loving kindness lasts forever. You are faithful to me and to my family. I give You all my praise because You are every joy, every triumph, and every good thing in my life.

You are Jehovah, the Lord, God all-powerful.

Reflection:

"Sometimes you will never know the value of a moment until it becomes a memory." – DR. SEUSS

Memory and Cognition:

Joy of Remembering

Share your thoughts in the sunshine images provided.

Take time to remember special moments.

What's your earliest memory?

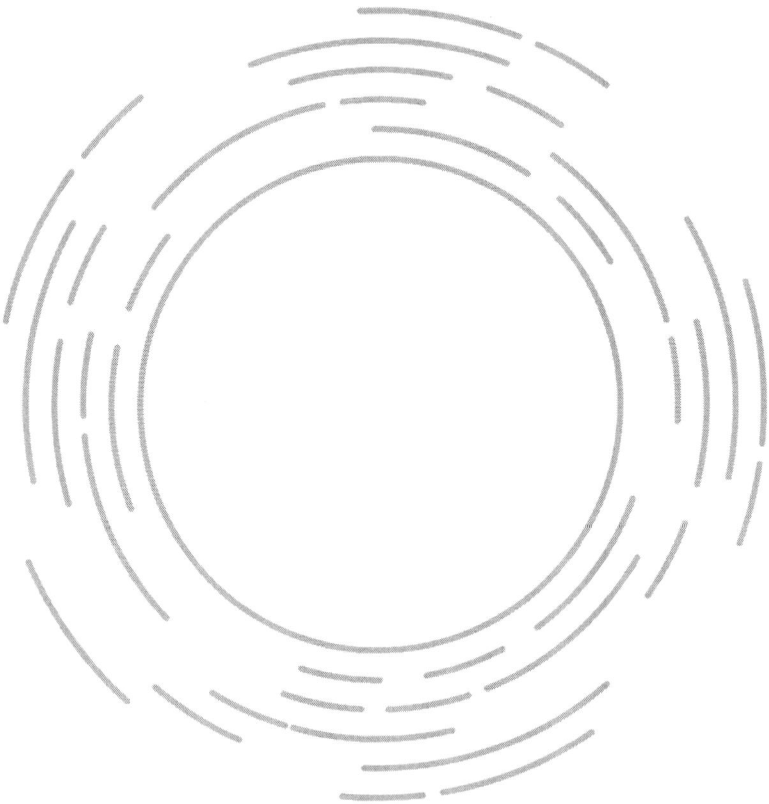

What has been your favorite age so far?
Share your story of why this age was special.

What is your favorite place, and how does it reflect the joy of the summer season of life?

What was your most memorable family vacation?

Remember a time that you couldn't stop laughing? Share that memory.

Reflect on a wonderful summertime event that you wished you had treasured more deeply in the moment. It's moments like those that inspire us to embrace this present summer season as an opportunity to make every moment count.

Was there a time you were proud of yourself but didn't celebrate it? How can you celebrate it in this new summer season?

What is your favorite memory of one of your favorite people? How can you create a new moment today with that favorite person?

Craft a thank-you note to one person who has supported you in life, expressing to them what their support has meant to you and how it's helped you.

Notes

Notes

Notes

A Summer Prayer of *Petition* and *Blessing*

Inspired By Psalm 24, 60 & 61

Jehovah-Gador Milchamah – Mighty in battle

He is the King of shining greatness. The Lord is strong and powerful. The Lord is powerful in war.

Lift up your heads, O gates. Lift them up, O doors that last forever, and the King of shining greatness will come in. The Lord of all is the King of shining greatness; One Who is mighty in battle.

Lord, this earth is Yours, and all that is in it, the world and all who live in it. For You have built it upon the seas. You have set it in the valleys where rivers flow and on the mountains where Your shining greatness is displayed.

Who may climb the mountain of the Lord? And who may stand in His holy place? Only those whose hands and hearts are pure, who do not worship idols and never tell lies. They will receive the Lord's blessing and have a right relationship with God, their Savior.

Hear my cry. Listen to my prayer. I call to You from the end of the earth when my heart is weak. Lead me to the rock that is higher than I. I will receive what is good from You, Lord, for what is right and good only comes from the One Who saves me.

You are mighty in battle. It is You who has made the land shake and have torn it open. Heal it where it is broken, for it shakes.

As I look for Your face, heal me and turn me toward You. For I also have suffered hard things. Save me with Your right hand and answer me so that I may be set free.

For You have been a safe place for me, a tower of strength where I am safe from those who fight against me. Let me live in Your tent forever. Let me be safe under the covering of Your wings. For You have heard my promises, O God. You have given me that which You give to those who fear Your name. Add days to my life so that I may sing thanks to Your name forever and keep my promises day by day.

Hear my cry, O God. Listen to my prayer. I call to You from the end of the earth when my heart is weak. Lead me to the rock that is higher than I. Let me see You in the sunrise and feel Your presence at sunset.

Response:

A Summer Prayer of *Petition* and *Blessing*

Highlight and respond below

Inspired By Psalm 24, 60 & 61

Jehovah-Gador Milchamah – Mighty in battle

___

___

He is the King of shining greatness. The Lord is strong and powerful. The Lord is powerful in war.

___

___

Lift up your heads, O gates. Lift them up, O doors that last forever, and the King of shining greatness will come in. The Lord of all is the King of shining greatness; One Who is mighty in battle.

___

___

___

Lord, this earth is Yours, and all that is in it, the world and all who live in it. For You have built it upon the seas. You have set it in the valleys where rivers flow and on the mountains where Your shining greatness is displayed.

Who may climb the mountain of the Lord? And who may stand in His holy place? Only those whose hands and hearts are pure, who do not worship idols and never tell lies. They will receive the Lord's blessing and have a right relationship with God, their Savior.

Hear my cry. Listen to my prayer. I call to You from the end of the earth when my heart is weak. Lead me to the rock that is higher than I. I will receive what is good from You, Lord, for what is right and good only comes from the One Who saves me.

You are mighty in battle. It is You who has made the land shake and have torn it open. Heal it where it is broken, for it shakes.

As I look for Your face, heal me and turn me toward You. For I also have suffered hard things. Save me with Your right hand and answer me so that I may be set free.

For You have been a safe place for me, a tower of strength where I am safe from those who fight against me. Let me live in Your tent forever. Let me be safe under the covering of Your wings. For You have heard my promises, O God. You have given me that which You give to those who fear Your name. Add days to my life so that I may sing thanks to Your name forever and keep my promises day by day.

Hear my cry, O God. Listen to my prayer. I call to You from the end of the earth when my heart is weak. Lead me to the rock that is higher than I. Let me see You in the sunrise and feel Your presence at sunset.

Reflection:

"Life begins at the end of your comfort zone."
– Neale Donald Walsh

"When the sun is shining, I can do anything; no mountain is too high, no trouble too difficult to overcome."
– Wilma Rudolph

Personal Growth:

Joy Outside the Comfort Zone

The concept that life begins when you step outside of your comfort zone has become widely understood and appreciated. Staying within the limits of what we know can often make us feel bored with life. If fear is the core reason we avoid trying new things, we risk becoming frustrated that we're allowing fear to hold us back from the life we dream of. Have you become so used to staying within your comfort zone that you've stopped thinking about what could be outside of it?

Reflect on your experience of living within your comfort zone.

When we overcome something that scares us, we not only feel a great sense of joy and accomplishment; we also increase our resilience and feel more confident about tackling future challenges. There is personal growth, new experiences, new people and memories, adaptability to change, and unlocking your full potential. But most importantly, we see God show up in our lives and give us what we need to accomplish the uncomfortable. The result: We experience the joys of living outside the comfort zone.

As Arianna Huffington says, *"The journey toward self-discovery is life's greatest adventure."* Congratulations on the greatest adventure of self-discovery outside your comfort zone in this summer season:

Which of your aspirations and dreams have you finally experienced because you had the courage to step outside of your comfort zone? Has this experience helped bring a summer season to your life?

Stepping out doesn't have to be big. It can come in life's smaller moments. Choose from the experiences listed, or note one of your own to reflect and write on the influence it had in a summer season.

- Introduced yourself to someone new
- Tried a new recipe
- Had open and honest conversations with someone around you
- Decided to be more spontaneous
- Tried a new outfit or hairstyle
- Tried a new workout routine
- Hiked or biked a new trail
- Invited new neighbors or acquaintances over

- Changed career paths
- Changed up your daily routine
- Developed a new skill
- Adjusted your financial budget
- Bought your dream home in a new neighborhood

What were you afraid of? What fears did you have on your path toward your aspirations/dreams?

Because you didn't let fear hold you back, how has stepping into the uncomfortable to accomplish these aspirations brought joy to life?

Write an elevator pitch to anyone who chooses to stay in their comfort zone, but needs to go to the Uncomfortable.

Notes

Notes

Notes

Notes

A Summer Song of *Worship* and *Praise*

Inspired By Psalm 97 & 98

Jehovah-Adon Kal Ha'arets -The Lord of all the Earth – Joshua 3:13

God's Power is over the Earth: A Call to Praise the Lord

Jehovah, You are King! Let the earth be full of joy with me.

Let the many islands be glad. It is amazing to me that even the clouds at sunrise and darkness at sunset surround You. My strength comes from the foundation of Your throne that is built upon what is right and fair.

Sing a brand new song to the Lord.

I will sing from my heart as I know that You have done great things in my life. I have experienced Your saving power. You are all that is good and right. Your loving kindness is beautiful to me.

All the earth calls out for joy to the Lord. Join me in song. Sing songs of great joy and praise. Sing praises to the Lord with all that you possess and with your voice.

Fire blazes out before You. Even Your lightning lights up the world. The earth sees and shakes. The mountains melt like a candle before You, the Lord of the whole earth. The heavens tell about how right and good You are. And everyone will see Your shining greatness.

Shout praises to the Lord.

You are my King, and I will continue to sing of your greatness. The world joins with me in praise to You, mighty God. The seas' waves make a loud noise, the rivers rushing waters clap, and the mountains rise to praise You. You will return to put the world and everyone in it right.

I will worship the one true God.

I am full of joy. For You are the Lord Most High over all the earth. You are to be honored above all. I love you, Lord. This love for Your righteousness causes me to hate what is bad. For You keep safe the souls of Your faithful ones. Light is spread like seed for those who are right and good. I will be glad in You, Who is right and good. I will give thanks to Your Holy name today and every day of my life.

Response:

A Summer Song of *Worship* and *Praise*

Highlight and respond below

Inspired By Psalm 97 & 98

Jehovah-Adon Kal Ha'arets – The Lord of all the Earth
–Joshua 3:13

God's Power is over the Earth: A Call to Praise the Lord

Jehovah, You are King! Let the earth be full of joy with me. Let the many islands be glad. It is amazing to me that even the clouds at sunrise and darkness at sunset surround You. My strength comes from the foundation of Your throne that is built upon what is right and fair.

Sing a brand new song to the Lord.

I will sing from my heart as I know that You have done great things in my life. I have experienced Your saving power. You are all that is good and right. Your loving kindness is beautiful to me.

All the earth calls out for joy to the Lord. Join me in song. Sing songs of great joy and praise. Sing praises to the Lord with all that you possess and with your voice.

Fire blazes out before You. Even Your lightning lights up the world. The earth sees and shakes. The mountains melt like a candle before You, the Lord of the whole earth. The heavens tell about how right and good You are. And everyone will see Your shining greatness.

Shout praises to the Lord

You are my King, and I will continue to sing of your greatness. The world joins with me in praise to You, mighty God. The seas' waves make a loud noise, the rivers rushing waters clap, and the mountains rise to praise You. You will return to put the world and everyone in it right.

I will worship the one true God.

I am full of joy. For You are the Lord Most High over all the earth. You are to be honored above all. I love you, Lord.

This love for Your righteousness causes me to hate what is bad. For You keep safe the souls of Your faithful ones. Light is spread like seed for those who are right and good. I will be glad in You, Who is right and good. I will give thanks to Your Holy name today and every day of my life.

Reflection:

> *"People will forget what you said, People will forget what you did, but People will never forget how you made them feel."*
> – MAYA ANGELOU

> *"If you see someone without a smile today, give 'em yours."*
> – DOLLY PARTON

Stress Management:

Joy of a Smile

Reflect and share your thoughts in the sunshine images.

Are you compelled to be the reason someone smiles today? Smiles are understood as a sign of friendliness, trust, authenticity, agreement, and social politeness.

Why is it important to smile?

Are smiles really contagious?

How can I remind myself to smile more?

I think smiles help people to…

If everyone smiled more,
the world would…

Think of the times you have shared a smile. Smiles can also be a sign of embarrassment, love, joy, happiness, general well being, amusement or contentment.

How often do you smile?

What does
your smile say?

How does smiling
make you feel?

When someone smiles at you,
you know...

Smiling feels good because...

Notes

Notes

Notes

A Summer Prayer of *Petition* and *Blessing*

Inspired By Psalm 67, 80 & 85

A Prayer for the Nation

O God of all, bring us back to You. Make Your face shine upon us and give us life again.

O Shepherd of Israel. The One Who sits on Your heavenly throne above the angels, let Your light shine! Stir up Your power, and come to save us! O Lord, You showed favor to Your land. It has produced its fruit. You have forgiven the sins of Your people. You have covered all their sin.

O God of all, show us Your loving kindness, and save us. Bring us back to life again so Your people may be happy in You.

Your saving power is near those who fear You so Your shining greatness may live in the land. Loving kindness and truth have met together. Peace and what is good and true have kissed each other. Truth comes up from the earth.

From heaven comes all goodness. Yes, Lord, You will give what is good, and our land will give its fruit. What is right and good will go before You and make a way for Your steps.

O God of all, I beg Your return. Look down from heaven, and see us. Give us new life again, and we will call on Your name.

Please bring us back to You. Make Your face shine upon us, and grace us with Your presence that we may receive our salvation. Show Your loving kindness toward us, and bring good into our lives once again. May Your way be known on the earth and Your saving power among all nations. May the people praise You, O God. May the nations be glad and sing for joy.

For You will be fair when You judge the people and rule the nations of the earth. May the people praise You.

O God of all, bring us back to You. Make Your face shine upon us and grant us our salvation so we may have life again.

Response:

A Summer Prayer of *Petition* and *Blessing*

Inspired By Psalm 67, 80 & 85

Highlight and respond below

A Prayer for the Nation

O God of all, bring us back to You. Make Your face shine upon us and give us life again.

O Shepherd of Israel. The One Who sits on Your heavenly throne above the angels, let Your light shine! Stir up Your power, and come to save us! O Lord, You showed favor to Your land. It has produced its fruit. You have forgiven the sins of Your people. You have covered all their sin.

O God of all, show us Your loving kindness, and save us. Bring us back to life again so Your people may be happy in You.

Your saving power is near those who fear You so Your shining greatness may live in the land. Loving kindness and truth have met together. Peace and what is good and true have kissed each other. Truth comes up from the earth.

From heaven comes all goodness. Yes, Lord, You will give what is good and our land will give its fruit. What is right and good will go before You and make a way for Your steps.

O God of all, I beg Your return. Look down from heaven, and see us. Give us new life again, and we will call on Your name.

Please bring us back to You. Make Your face shine upon us, and grace us with Your presence that we may receive our salvation. Show Your loving kindness toward us, and bring good into our lives once again. May Your way be known on the earth and Your saving power among all nations. May the people praise You, O God. May the nations be glad and sing for joy.

For You will be fair when You judge the people and rule the nations of the earth. May the people praise You.

O God of all, bring us back to You. Make Your face shine upon us and grant us our salvation so we may have life again.

Reflection:

> *"Freedom is the open window through which pours the sunlight of the human spirit and human dignity."* – HERBERT HOOVER

Empowerment:

Joy of Freedom

What does freedom personally mean to you?

____

____

How has your freedom driven you to contribute to society?

____

____

What do you think about social media as you consider freedom?

____

____

Reflect on Herbert Hoover's quote. Which freedom has had the greatest positive impact in your world?

____

____

____

____

____

Reflect on the freedoms you enjoy – from the time you wake up to the time you go to sleep – that have brought joyful living. Write the freedoms that are most meaningful to you within each category.

Spiritual Freedom

Mental Freedom

Physical Freedom

Emotional Freedom

Notes

Notes

Notes

A SUMMER SONG OF *Worship* AND *Praise*

INSPIRED BY PSALM 104 & 46

Jehovah-Bara—The Everlasting God, the Lord, Creator of the ends of the earth

Come and see the works of the Lord. Be quiet, and know that I am God. I will be honored in the earth. The Lord of All is with us.

Praise the Lord, O my soul! My God is great, beautiful, and gloriously robed. He is dressed in sunshine with great honor and wonderful power. Come and see the works of the Lord. Be quiet, and know that He is God. He will be honored among the nations. He will be honored in the earth. The Lord of All is with me.

God has set the earth in its place so that it will stay that way forever. He covered it with the sea and made the waters stand above the mountains. The waters left at His strong words. They dispersed quickly at the sound of His thunder. The mountains rose up, and the valleys came down to the place that He made for them. God set a place that they may not pass over. The waters will never cover the earth again, and God made this promise for me.

God sent rivers into the valleys to flow between the mountains, giving water to all the animals of the field and the birds of the sky. He waters the mountains from His heavenly home, and the earth is filled with the fruit of His works. And He did this all for me.

Come and see the works of the Lord. Be quiet, and know that He is God. He will be honored in the earth. The Lord of All is with me.

As happy faces glow with health, they are a people well fed and hearty. God's trees are well watered. Birds build their nests in those trees; mountain goats climb about the cliffs; badgers burrow among the rocks. The moon keeps track of the seasons, and the sun is in charge of each day. God makes darkness, and it becomes night so all the wild animals among the trees can venture out. The deep, wide sea is brimming with fish past counting, and He did this all for me.

Come and see the works of the Lord. Be quiet, and know that He is God. He will be honored in the earth. The Lord of All is with me.

What a wildly wonderful world God has made! He made it all for me, with wisdom at His side. May His shining greatness last forever. I will sing to the Lord all my life. I will sing praise to Him as long as I live. May the words of my heart be pleasing to Him. As for me, I will be glad in the Lord, and I am so thankful. Let everything inside me Praise the Lord, for He did this all for me.

Response:

A Summer Song of *Worship* and *Praise*

Highlight and respond below

Inspired By Psalm 104 & 46

Jehovah-Bara – The Everlasting God, the Lord, Creator of the ends of the earth

____

____

COME and see the works of the Lord. Be quiet, and know that I am God. I will be honored in the earth. The Lord of All is with us.

____

____

Praise the Lord, O my soul! My God is great, beautiful, and gloriously robed. He is dressed in sunshine with great honor and wonderful power. Come and see the works of the Lord. Be quiet, and know that He is God. He will be honored among the nations. He will be honored in the earth. The Lord of All is with me.

____

____

God has set the earth in its place so that it will stay that way forever. He covered it with the sea and made the waters stand above the mountains. The waters left at His strong words. They dispersed quickly at the sound of His thunder. The mountains rose up, and the valleys came down to the place that He made for them. God set a place that they may not pass over. The waters will never cover the earth again, and God made this promise for me.

God sent rivers into the valleys to flow between the mountains, giving water to all the animals of the field and the birds of the sky. He waters the mountains from His heavenly home, and the earth is filled with the fruit of His works. And He did this all for me.

Come and see the works of the Lord. Be quiet, and know that He is God. He will be honored in the earth. The Lord of All is with me.

As happy faces glow with health, they are a people well fed and hearty. God's trees are well watered. Birds build their nests in those trees; mountain goats climb about the cliffs; badgers burrow among the rocks. The moon keeps track of the seasons, and the sun is in charge of each day. God makes darkness, and it becomes night so all the wild animals among the trees can venture out. The deep, wide sea is brimming with fish past counting, and He did this all for me.

Come and see the works of the Lord. Be quiet, and know that He is God. He will be honored in the earth. The Lord of All is with me.

What a wildly wonderful world God has made! He made it all for me, with wisdom at His side. May His shining greatness last forever. I will sing to the Lord all my life. I will sing praise to Him as long as I live. May the words of my heart be pleasing to Him. As for me, I will be glad in the Lord, and I am so thankful. Let everything inside me Praise the Lord, for He did this all for me.

Reflection:

The summer sun fiercely makes its presence known, allowing for the days to be longer and to expose our true and fragile selves. We cannot hide in the summer season with the sun sharing its glory, vitality, and keenness of vision. This season shares its heart with us as we dance to our new discoveries. – MARY KATHLEEN

Sunlight, blue skies, abundance of green, singing birds, and longer evenings are definitely things that make the summer seem more alive. – KRISTEN

Emotional Expression:

Joy in New Discoveries

We cannot hide in the summer season with the sun sharing its glory, vitality, and keenness of vision. This season shares its heart with us as we dance to our new discoveries. Follow the prompts to craft your responses noting the ways you've stretched yourself, then reflect on the emotion you feel in that discovery. Write within the sunshine images.

You tried something new:

You *dance in this new discovery* with

You pushed yourself to a new limit:

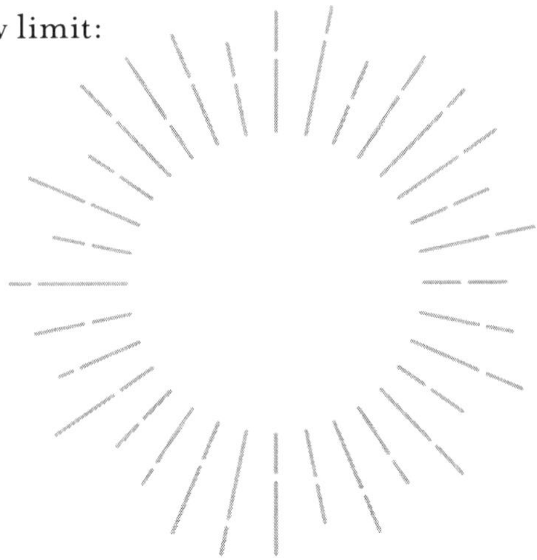

You *dance in this new discovery* with

You discovered something new about yourself:

You *dance in this new discovery* with

You became keenly aware of nature and its beauty:

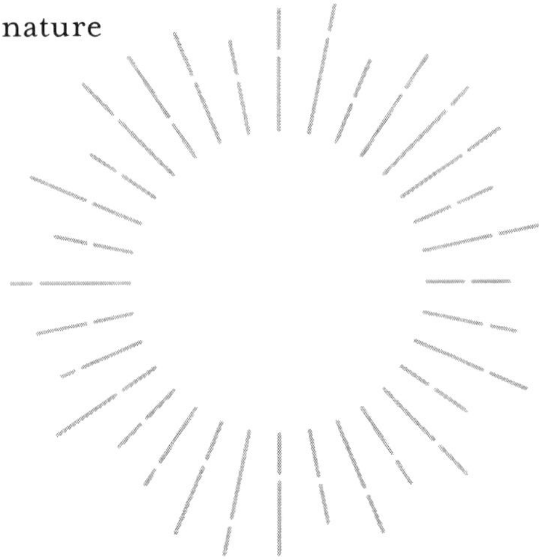

You *dance in this new discovery* with

You discovered something new about your world:

You *dance in this new discovery* with

You discovered something new about faith:

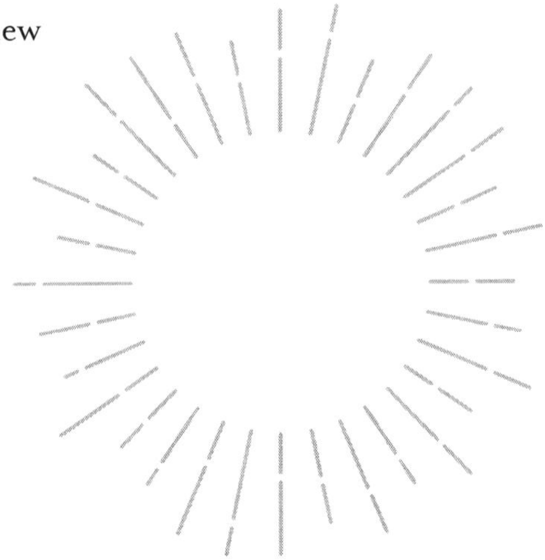

You *dance in this new discovery* with

In a wildly wonderful world that God has made just for you, what was something you longed to hear? Express how it made you feel more alive when you heard it.

What was something you longed to see? Express how it made you feel more alive when you saw it.

Notes

Notes

Notes

Notes

A Summer Prayer of *Petition* and *Blessing*

Inspired By Psalms 109 & 63

Jehovah-Rophe – Healer

"He was wounded for our transgressions,
He was bruised for our iniquities;
The chastisement for our peace was upon Him,
And by His stripes we are healed." – Isaiah 53:5

O Lord my God, be kind to me because of Your name.

Take me out of this trouble because Your loving kindness is good. For I am in need, and my heart is hurting. My knees are weak because I have not eaten for days, and my body has lost weight. No one understands my troubles. People laugh at me. They look at me and shake their heads. They think there is no hope for me.

Help me, O Lord my God! Save me by Your loving kindness.

Let those who speak against me know that my help is from Your hand alone. Let this bring hope to them. When bad things happen to them, they will know that You are the One that makes good things happen.

I will look for You with all my heart and strength. My soul is thirsty for You. My flesh is weak, wanting You in a dry and tired land where there is no water. I have seen You in the holy place. I have seen Your power and Your shining greatness.

O Lord my God, be kind to me because of Your name.

I will be full of joy for the goodness that You have shown me. I will give thanks to You in a loud voice, and I will praise You. My lips will praise You because Your loving kindness is better than life. I will give honor to You as long as I live. I will lift up my hands in Your name. My soul will be filled, as with rich foods, and my mouth will praise You with lips of joy.

If I'm sleepless at midnight, I spend the hours in grateful reflection because you have always stood up for me. In the darkness, I will sing a song, and I'm completely full of joy! Everything inside of me clings to you because you emotionally lift me up.

O Lord my God, continue to be kind to me because of Your name.

I'm free to run and play. I hold on to you for dear life as you hold me steady.

Response:

A Summer Prayer of *Petition* and *Blessing*

Highlight and respond below

Inspired By Psalm 109 & 63

Jehovah-Rophe – Healer

"He was wounded for our transgressions,
He was bruised for our iniquities;
The chastisement for our peace was upon Him,
And by His stripes we are healed." – Isaiah 53:5

O Lord my God, be kind to me because of Your name.

Take me out of this trouble because Your loving kindness is good. For I am in need, and my heart is hurting. My knees are weak because I have not eaten for days, and my body has lost weight. No one understands my troubles. People laugh at me. They look at me and shake their heads. They think there is no hope for me.

Help me, O Lord my God! Save me by Your loving kindness. Let those who speak against me know that my help is from Your hand alone. Let this bring hope to them. When bad things happen to them, they will know that You are the One that makes good things happen.

I will look for You with all my heart and strength. My soul is thirsty for You. My flesh is weak, wanting You in a dry and tired land where there is no water. I have seen You in the holy place. I have seen Your power and Your shining greatness.

O Lord my God, be kind to me because of Your name. I will be full of joy for the goodness that You have shown me. I will give thanks to You in a loud voice, and I will praise You. My lips will praise You because Your loving kindness is better than life. I will give honor to You as long as I live. I will lift up my hands in Your name. My soul will be filled, as with rich foods, and my mouth will praise You with lips of joy.

If I'm sleepless at midnight, I spend the hours in grateful reflection because you have always stood up for me. In the darkness, I will sing a song, and I'm completely full of joy! Everything inside of me clings to you because you emotionally lift me up.

O Lord my God, continue to be kind to me because of Your name. I'm free to run and play. I hold on to you for dear life as you hold me steady.

Reflection:

"The mere sense of living is joy enough." —EMILY DICKINSON

"Do what you can with what you have, where you are."
— THEODORE ROOSEVELT

Memory and Cognitive:

Joy of Gathering

In Hebrews 10:24, there is a command to not neglect gathering together: "Let us consider one another in order to provoke love and good works, not neglecting to gather together, as some are in the habit of doing, but encouraging each other."

According to Mayo Health systems, there are many benefits to gathering. When we come together and share experiences, thoughts and ideas, we gain empathy and understanding for one another. This helps us better understand the world around us and how our actions can impact others. Ultimately, togetherness gives us the strength and support we need to succeed. Not only is gathering together enjoyable, but it also nurtures our most important relationships and promotes a sense of belonging and community.

Benefits to gathering can include:

- Creating close relationships
- Emotional support
- Preventing isolation
- Improving confidence and self-worth
- Acceptance
- Improving health and well-being
- A sense of purpose
- Boosting happiness
- Reducing stress
- Enriching your life

From sunrise through sunset, this summer season has never been a better time to gather with the ones you hold dearest.

Write about an experience of sharing a meal and the benefits gained in this gathering.

____

____

____

____

____

When did playing games or participating in an activity or a sport show you the benefits of gathering?

____

____

____

____

____

Think of a fun-filled vacation shared with friends or family. What benefits came from experiencing a vacation together?

Which small group are you a part of? What are the benefits of gathering regularly with this group?

Was there a party or celebration that brought so much joy? Describe the benefits you felt during and after this gathering.

Write an elevator pitch to someone who chooses isolation, and convince them of the enormous benefits of gathering with community, friends, family, neighbors and colleagues.

Notes

Notes

Notes

A Summer Song of *Worship* and *Praise*

Inspired By Psalm 95

Jehovah-Kanna — Lord Jealous

A Song of Praise

"I must worship no other gods, but only Jehovah, for He is God who claims absolute loyalty and exclusive devotion." — Exodus 34:14

With a thankful heart, I will sing loudly and joyfully to the Rock Who saved me. With delight, I will make a sound of joy to Him through song. For the Lord is a great God, and the great King above all gods. The deepest places of the earth are in His hands, and the tops of the mountains belong to Him. The sea is His and His hands made the dry land. He made it all for my enjoyment.

For God is the Creator of all good things, and I am in awe of His beautiful creations.

With a grateful heart, I bow down in worship. Daily, I will humble myself, getting down on my knees before the Lord to worship the One who made me. For He is our God, and we are the people of His field and the sheep of His hand. If you hear His voice today, do not let your heart become hard. Sing a joyous, thankful song to Him, the God of our salvation.

For the Lord is a great God, and the great King above all gods

Response

A Summer Song of *Worship* and *Praise*

Highlight and respond below

Inspired By Psalm 95

Jehovah-Kanna – Lord Jealous

A Song of Praise

"I must worship no other gods, but only Jehovah, for He is God who claims absolute loyalty and exclusive devotion." – Exodus 34:14

WITH a thankful heart, I will sing loudly and joyfully to the Rock Who saved me. With delight, I will make a sound of joy to Him through song. For the Lord is a great God, and the great King above all gods. The deepest places of the earth are in His hands, and the tops of the mountains belong to Him. The sea is His and His hands made the dry land. He made it all for my enjoyment.

For God is the Creator of all good things and I am in awe of His beautiful creations.

With a grateful heart, I bow down in worship. Daily I will humble myself, getting down on my knees before the Lord to worship the One who made me. For He is our God and we are the people of His field and the sheep of His hand. If you hear His voice today, do not let your heart become hard. Sing a joyous, thankful song to Him, the God of our salvation.

For the Lord is a great God, and the great King above all gods.

Reflection

"Turn your face to the Sun, and the shadows fall behind you."
– MÁORI PROVERB

"The past is frozen and no longer flows, and the present is all lit up with eternal rays." – C.S. LEWIS

Gratitude:

Joy in the Sunrise and Sunset

His sunrises cast diamonds on the water as it moves; His sunsets are painted warm in tangerine hues; and we gain a glimpse of the artistic beauty we'll one day experience for all eternity. We experience God's goodness in the flowers, birds, water and grass beneath our feet. Reflect on the beauty that surrounds you and know this is the celebration of all you've worked long for.

The past is frozen and no longer flows. Do you feel life is going too fast, just right, or too slow?

Turn your face to the Sun. How would you describe this morning's sunrise?

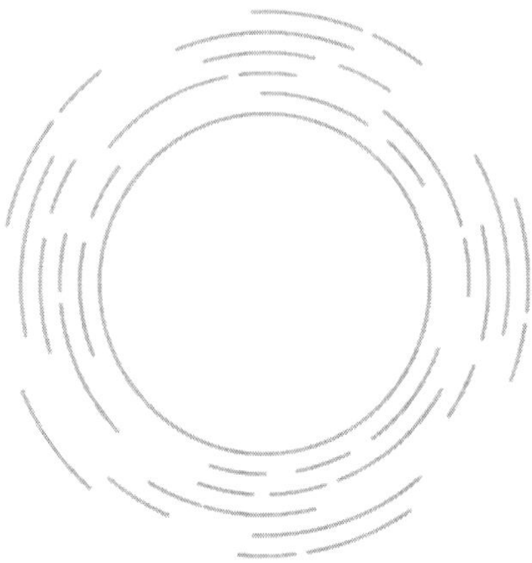

The present moment is all lit up with eternal rays. How do you intend to celebrate the warmth of this sunshine season?

Turning your face to the Sonshine (God's ever-presence) today, how has this allowed for *the shadows to fall behind you*?

How would you describe this evening's sunset?

Share your thoughts of gratitude as you take in the beauty of the sunset.

As you turn your face to the sunset this evening, share what has brought you to a place of gratitude and anticipation for the celebration that awaits you tomorrow.

Notes

Notes

Notes

Notes

The Prayer of the *Lord*

Matthew 6: 9 - 13

In this manner, therefore, pray.

Our Father in heaven,
Hallowed be Your name.
Your Kingdom come.
Your Will be done
On earth as it is in heaven.
Give us this day our daily bread.
And forgive us our debts,
As we forgive our debtors.
And do not lead us into temptation,
But deliver us from the evil one.
For Yours is the kingdom and the power and the glory forever.
Amen

Response:

The Prayer of the *Lord*

Highlight and respond below

MATTHEW 6: 9 - 13

In this manner, therefore, pray.

OUR Father in heaven,
Hallowed be Your name.
Our Father in heaven, Reveal who you are.

Your Kingdom come.
Set the world right;

Your Will be done
On earth as it is in heaven.
Do what's best— as above, so below.

Give us this day our daily bread.
Keep us alive with three square meals.

And forgive us our debts,
As we forgive our debtors.
Keep us forgiven with you and forgiving others.

And do not lead us into temptation,
But deliver us from the evil one.
Keep us safe from ourselves and the Devil.

For Yours is the kingdom and the power and the glory forever.

Amen.

You're in charge! You can do anything you want! You're ablaze in beauty! Yes. Yes. Yes. – MATTHEW 6:7-13 (MSG)

Reflection:

> *"The Bible is not an end in itself, but a means to bring men to an intimate and satisfying knowledge of God, that they may enter into Him, that they may delight in His presence, may taste and know the inner sweetness of the very God Himself in the core and center of their hearts."* – A.W. Toser

> *"They who pray with faith have fervor, and fervor is the fire of prayer. This mysterious fire has the power of consuming all our faults and imperfections, and of giving to our actions; vitality, beauty and merit."* – St. Frances Xavier Cabrini

Personal Growth:

Joy of Solitude

Reflect on a joyful time of solitude. Where do you experience the joy of solitude wherein you *delight in His presence*, and *know the inner sweetness of the very God Himself in the core and center of your heart*? Reflect and write about this precious time of peace, quiet, loveliness and goodness. Describe what you feel and see.

A fervent prayer is filled with passion, persistence and power. It is a prayer that comes from a heart that is fully devoted to God and His purposes. Prayer is the most direct way to sincerely speak to God, to adore Him, to confess one's shortcomings, to thank Him, to petition Him for needs or just to connect with our heavenly Father about what is going on in life and in the world.

ACTS is a simple acrostic. It's a guide to prayer. Each letter stands for one of the key elements of prayer:

Adoration

Confession

Thanksgiving

Supplication

A.C.T.S. will enrich your quiet time. It will give freedom to have a common everyday conversation with God; a conversation that's intimate, loving, and honest. A.C.T.S. will give your personal, quiet-time prayer more depth and meaning. You will be focused on being thankful instead of needy. When we take time to honor God for whom He is and to praise Him for all He has done, our adoration of Him will grow even more.

Use this acrostic tool to write out your prayer in this delightful summer season of life represented by the joys of living from sunrise to sunset.

In Genesis 32:9 you can read Jacob's ACTS of prayer. Jacob begins by praising God for who He is: Jacob said, "O God of my father Abraham and God of my father Isaac..."

God's Word says that if you have unconfessed sin, God literally cannot hear your prayers until you confess. So, Jacob confesses: "I am not worthy of the least of all the mercies and of all the truth which You have shown Your servant..."

Jacob gives thanks by listing the great things God has done for him: "Kindness, faithfulness God has shown me," And he says, "...for I crossed over this Jordan with my staff, and now I have become two companies."

Jacob requests that God save him and his family from his brother. "Deliver me, I pray, from the hand of my brother, from the hand of Esau; for I fear him, lest he come and attack me and the mother with the children."

Follow the guidance below to write your prayer.

A is for Adoration: A time of praising God for Who He is. His attributes, His name and His character.

God, you are...

____

____

____

____

C is for Confession: A time to confess your sins and to ask forgiveness. When you come into His presence, remember times you have come short of His holiness.

God, I am sorry for...

____

____

____

____

T is for Thanksgiving: A time to thank God for the grace and mercy He has shown you.

Thank you God for...

S is for Supplication: A time to bring your requests for the needs of others and yourself to God.

God, please will You...

Notes

Notes

Notes

Notes

Time for Everything

There is a time for everything, and a season for every activity
under the heavens;

a time to be born and a time to die,

a time to plant and a time to uproot,

a time to kill and a time to heal,

a time to tear down and a time to build,

a time to weep and a time to laugh,

a time to mourn and a time to dance,

a time to scatter stones and a time to gather them,

a time to embrace and a time to refrain from embracing,

a time to search and a time to give up,

a time to keep and a time to throw away, a time to tear
and a time to mend,

a time to be silent and a time to speak,

a time to love and a time to hate,

a time for war and a time for peace.

– Ecclesiastes 3:1-8

Acknowledgements

I am especially grateful to those wonderful friends who shared their stories and sentiments in "Sunrise to Sunset" that brought incredible insight and passion to this project. Thank you to Angie, Carmen, Kristin, Mary Kathleen, and Michelle.

My thanks also goes to my family for their encouragement, involvement, and support. A special love goes to my littles who call me Nana; I treasure our time together and have inserted every lesson learned into this project. And to my husband, Paul: You always believe in me. Thank you.

TO CONTACT THE AUTHOR

Bonnie Liabenow is a passionate, committed, faith – driven woman. She is dedicated to providing encouragement in words of faith to women of all ages during all seasons of their lives. She has counseled women across the country in personal goal-setting, goal acquisition, and time management. Bonnie has also demonstrated a commitment to service, hard work and excellence through her professional career. In addition to serving her community as an author and teacher, she is also the Vice President of Core Communications International , and has been recognized as a successful 'Lady Farmer' by various reputable publications for her strides and best practices in the Christmas Tree farming industry. Prior to launching her professional career, she finished two years of biblical studies at Bethel College, and earned a bachelor of science degree in recreational therapy at Michigan State University. Bonnie is a proud wife, mother of three sons / two daughter-in-laws and finds complete joy in being 'Nana' to her six grandchildren.

Bonnie Liabenow is an inspirational speaker/life coach who delivers a powerful emotional message to women of faith. Invite Bonnie to lead your group to live intentionally, and to experience a new day with purpose and fulfillment.

Contact Bonnie at bliabenow@live.com
or at facebook.com/bonnieliabenow

Also by Bonnie Liabenow

Excellence with Simple Elegance

And it's companion workbook

The Study

JOURNALING THROUGH THE SEASONS

The new series of guided journals

Journaling through the Seasons: Fall & Faith

Journaling through the Seasons: Winter & Word

Journaling through the Seasons: Spring & Spirit

Journaling through the Seasons: Summer & Sonship